TAXI JUBILEE

Fifty Years of the Austin FX4 London Taxi

Bill Munro

Earlswood Press

First published in 2009 by Earlswood Press, 10 Chaldon Close, Redhill, Surrey RH1 6SX

British Library Cataloguing-in-Publication Data
A catalogue record for this book is available from the British Library.

ISBN 978-0-9562308-0-5

Typset by Earlswood Press

Printed and bound in Great Britain by Lavenham Press, Water Street, Lavenham, Sudbury, Suffolk CO10 9RN

Sole distributor:
Vintage Taxi Spares, Dairy House Farm, Front Street, East Stour, Nr Gillingham, Dorset SP8 5LQ
www.vintagetaxispares.com

Contents

Acknowledgments

The author wishes to extend grateful thanks to the following people for their help in the production of this book:

From the London cab trade: Stuart Pessok, Taxi Newspaper; Stanley Roth; Steve Tillyer; the late Geoff Trotter of the London General Cab Company.

From LTI, Mann and Overton, Austin and Carbodies: Eric Bailey; Maria Holmes-Wood; Peter James; Grant Lockhart; the late Bill Lucas; Ed Osmond; Andrew Overton; Updesh Ramnath; Jevon Thorpe; Barry Widdowson; the late Peter Wildgoose

From the London Vintage Taxi Association and other historic vehicle clubs: Anthony Blackman; Hans Dooren; Martin Hayter; Oliver Hyafil; Bob McPhail; Mal Smith; Graham Waite; Eddie Zetlein

Picture Credits:

Bart & Gujs de Bruijn, page 65 (both); Chris Forteath, page 63; the Imperial War Museum, page 50; Murray Jackson, pages 30 (centre), 35; The Worshipful Company of Hackney Carriage Drivers, pages 6, 8 (lower); Bryan Goodman, page 7; Andrew Hall, page 11; Olivier Hyafil, pages 44 (lower), 46 (upper); Imperial War Museum, 51; Sandra & Dean of the Classic Hearse Register, page 45; London Vintage Taxi Association, page 17; Stuart Pessok, Taxi Newspaper pages 29, 34, 50 (upper), 60, (both) 61, 62 (both); the Postal Museum and Archive, page 46; Bill Powell, page 48 (upper & middle); Stanley Roth, pages 15, 16, 25, 42 (centre & lower), 43 (both), 44 (upper), 47 (both) ; Barney Sharratt, pages 10, (middle & lower) 23, 27, 39, 42 (upper); Don Smith, page 30 (upper & lower); Vintage Taxi Spares, title page, pages 8 (upper), 50; London Taxis International, pages 23, 36, 40, 48, 49. Author's collection, 10 (upper). Remainder taken by the author

Image of Mettoy tin-plate model, page 54 reproduced by kind permission of Corgi

Introduction

Londoners may take the sight of their taxis for granted, but if asked if they thought that their longest-serving model, the Austin FX4 could be considered to be one of the world's most famous and most recognisable motor vehicles, few would disagree. There can hardly be a film or a television programme set in Britain's capital city in the later part of the twentieth century that doesn't at least show one or have a character stepping in or out of one these iconic vehicles. You can even recognise one by the noise it makes: hear, on a radio soundtrack the rattle of the engine, the squeal of the brakes and the slam of the doors and you know the character is getting out of a taxi. And it's not just any taxi- it's an Austin FX4.

The cab has been with us since the end of 1958, with November 2008 marking the golden jubilee of its service life. Production actually ended in 1997, but many of the last examples can, at the time of writing be seen carrying passengers in London and elsewhere in the UK and may well last for a few more years, as long as the legislation permits them to be licensed.

For it to have lasted so long, you might expect it to be an exceptional vehicle. In truth it wasn't that special as a piece of motor engineering, and compared to its predecessors it had some serious shortcomings. It was in fact intended to be made for just ten years, but it remained in production for all that time because there was never enough money to build a replacement.

In 1985, when killing off a proposed new model, the modern style CR6, its makers, the newly-formed London Taxis International tried to 'spin' the decision by saying that they '..had detected a preference... for the classic lines of the FX4 body styling.' They were prophetic words. It would be another three decades beyond its intended production life before that replacement, the TX1 was finally introduced, itself a homage to the FX4's familiar shape. And in that time, everyone grew to love the FX4 and to identify its familiar shape with London, acknowledging it as being as much of an icon of the city as Big Ben, the red buses and the guardsmen outside Buckingham Palace.

We aim here to tell the FX4's story: how it came about, what made it how it was and exactly why it lasted so long. We look too at examples that have been sold around the world, some famous and influential people who have bought them for their own private use, and many other versions; hire cars, hearses, vans and even stretch limousines. So having hailed us, so to speak, climb aboard and enjoy the ride!

Chapter 1
Before the FX4

For almost half the time it was in production, the FX4 London taxi carried Austin badges. Its two predecessors, the 12/4 and the FX3 did so for their entire lives and so most people with some interest in cars might assume that Austin had the idea of building these taxicabs, and that they built the FX4 entirely by themselves. But they'd be wrong: Austin became a major name in the manufacture of London taxicabs as long ago as 1929 through the initiative of London cab dealers Mann and Overton. And the FX4, like the FX3 before it, was not put together in Austin's factory in Birmingham, but in Coventry by Carbodies Ltd.

Mann and Overton's story goes back to 1898, when a young Tom Overton left his family's prosperous farm in Surrey and went to Paris to indulge his passion for a recent invention, the motor car. There he met a fellow Englishman, John J. Mann, who was already buying French and German cars and shipping them over to London to sell. The two joined forces to form Mann and Overton's Garage, acquiring premises in Pimlico, near London's Victoria Station. The young company's customers were the rich, who were the only people who could afford cars, but things would change when in 1903 a new, potentially huge market for motor cabs for London appeared: there were some 11,000 horse cabs in the capital, all of which might be replaced by motors.

In entering the London motor cab market, (we cannot say 'taxi' yet, because taximeters, the very item that gives a taxi, or taxicab its name would not be made mandatory in London until 1907) Mann and Overton's were entering a unique and, to the outsider totally mysterious world.

Far left: John James Mann. Sadly, Mann died in 1911 and would not see how his company would come to dominate the London taxi trade
Near left: J. T. 'Tom' Overton, who, with his brother, Will, ran Mann and Overton's until the mid-1920s

The licensing of London's horse cabs and cabmen was controlled by the Public Carriage Office, (PCO) a branch of the Metropolitan Police, based at New Scotland Yard. They were answerable only to the Home Office and ruled the trade with an iron hand. They wrote the rules governing the design of cabs and undertook annual inspections of the cabs prior to licensing them and made roadside inspections, removing those unfit for work. But the PCO was at a loss to know how to assess the bewildering variety of new motors submitted to them for approval, of which Mann and Overton's first offering, the Richard-Brasier was just one. In May, 1906, after consultation with some of the few experts that were around, the PCO introduced new regulations for motor cabs, the Conditions of Fitness, which prompted Mann and Overton's to change to another French vehicle, the Unic. It proved to be one of the best on the road and soon Mann and Overton's, who had found a flair for the business and established a rapport with the PCO cornered the London taxi market. However, supplies of the Unic ceased at the outbreak of the Great War. In 1920, after peace had resumed, Unic once more supplied Mann and Overton's with a revised version, but by 1926 it was all but finished, too antiquated and too expensive in the face of competition from two newcomers, Beardmore and Citroën.

The Conditions of Fitness had remained unchanged since their introduction, but just about everything else related to motor cars had changed profoundly, and most makers had no interest in making taxis for what was now, by comparison with ordinary motor car sales a tiny market. The rules were amended in 1927 to try to attract new makers and this was the incentive that Will Overton, Tom Overton's brother, who was now running the company needed to persuade Austin to make a taxi out of their best-selling 12/4 car. Throughout the 1930s, the Austin 12/4 taxicab dominated the London market, but by early 1940, after the outbreak of war, production ceased for good.

Austin valued their connection with the London cab trade; to have the public see their vehicles performing one of the toughest of urban tasks was a great advert for the company and after the war, Austin delivered a new prototype to Mann and Overton. From this, came the new

A Unic 12/16 of around 1912 vintage. Cabs like this would be seen in London until the late 1920s

An Austin 12/4 LL 'Low Loader', with a body by Strachan of Acton, West London. The Low Loader was made between 1934 and 1938

model of Austin taxicab, the FX3. Britain had been bankrupted by the war and the government urged all of the nations's industry to export everything it produced to earn foreign currency. Austin embraced this policy but the consequence of it was that they needed all their capacity to make car and truck bodies and could only supply the cab chassis. They could not build the body, let alone the complete cab, so somebody outside the company was needed to do the job. That would be Carbodies Ltd, of Coventry, who been in business since 1919, building bodies for MG, Hillman and many others. In such austere times, when work of any sort was welcome, the lure of a captive market with guaranteed sales was irresistible. But there would be a price to pay: Carbodies would contribute 25 percent of the finance, matching 25 percent from Austin, with the lion's share, 50 percent coming from the main sponsors, Mann and Overton.

Introduced in November 1948, the Austin FX3 proved to be as popular as the 12/4 before it. A diesel engine version, introduced in 1953 became an immediate success, with 90 percent of all subsequent FX3s sold being diesels. This engine, robust but slow, with a characteristic noise, and the standard black paint, set the image for London taxis that lasts to this day.

An Austin FX3. Over 7,500 were built between 1948 and 1958

Chapter 2
A Troubled Start

Life at both Austin and Carbodies changed a lot during the FX3's ten-year production run. Austin became the major partner in the British Motor Corporation and Carbodies was taken over by the massive BSA Group. Life at Mann and Overton, on the other hand changed little. They remained the biggest dealer of taxicabs in London and were still an independent, family business, run by Tom Overton's son, Robert Overton and his cousin, David Southwell and with the FX3, they had the London taxi market virtually to themselves. But the FX3 was already old-fashioned when new. By the mid-1950s it looked positively ancient compared to the sleek, pastel coloured cars produced by Vauxhall, Ford and indeed Austin and by 1956 it was due for replacement.

What should the new cab be like? Should it embody the traditional, even old-fashioned style of its predecessors, or would it be a new, ground-breaking design, incorporating all the latest technology? Its overall design was governed by the Conditions of Fitness, which would offer little scope for imaginative styling. Conservatism within the trade played a part too: putting something revolutionary into a cab, such as the front-wheel drive technology that would be used in the Mini (Austin had not begun to develop this for anything larger) would be a gamble that would be rejected as too expensive to buy and too difficult to maintain.

London cabs are built for a service life of ten years and so it made sense to have a conservative design rather than to follow fashion. Austin's chief stylist, Ricardo 'Dick' Burzi had been with the company since the 1920s, when he was forced to leave his native Italy after insulting the country's fascist dictator, Benito Mussolini. Busy with other work, he passed the job of designing the new cab to Eric Bailey, an assistant in the body engineering department. Bailey, in an interview with motoring journalist Barney Sharratt, said he; '... didn't envisage anything too radical, just a pleasant shape that would cause no offence to anyone.'

Bailey's first design had three doors, like the FX3, but it was Mr. Gould, the Principal of the PCO who recommended the fitting of a fourth door across the luggage platform. Bailey went back to his drawing board and produced some variations of the shape that would become one of the world's most recognisable, most famous motor vehicles. It wasn't like anything Dick Burzi had designed, or what Austin would introduce a couple of years on with the 'Farina' A40, but something of a modernisation of the big Austin Princess limousine that Bailey had

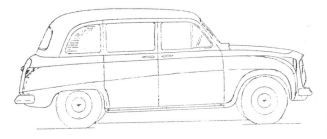

One of Eric Bailey's early drafts, showing the faired in headlights and a very different wing shape

worked on a few years before. In other words, a timeless, understated shape, very British in its character. Its first designation, in BMC's new system was ADO6, but soon it was called, under Austin's old numbering system, FX4. Bailey's drawings were passed to Carbodies, where body engineer Jake Donaldson turned the design into working drawings for the body pressings that would be assembled into a complete vehicle. He took care to ensure that the body could be easily and quickly repaired, designing bolt-on front and rear wings and door sills. All the interior trim panels were one-piece plastic mouldings, easy to clean and to replace if damaged.

Austin produced a serviceable chassis, using suspension and brakes from its big Westminster saloon car and the diesel engine from the FX3 that had proven itself beyond doubt. During the

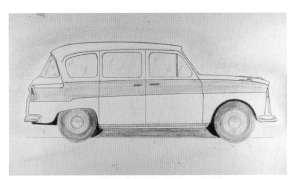

last few years of the FX3's life, London cab proprietors had asked Mann and Overton if cabs could be fitted with automatic gearboxes, which

Above: a wrap-around rear window was one idea that Mann and Overton did not accept; cost was probably a major consideration. Eric Bailey used two-tone colours to add a some extra interest
Left: this was the design that Robert Overton and David Southwell of Mann & Overton decided upon

were beginning to be seen on larger cars in Britain. They were fed up with always having to fit new clutches, as older cabmen, brought up on crash gearboxes would slip the clutch constantly rather than change gear, wearing the clutch out far too quickly. An automatic gearbox was tested in a small number of FX3s and proved to be satisfactory, and so an automatic was all that was fitted to the cab.

Representatives of the London cab trade were invited to Carbodies' factory in Coventry in June 1958 to view the new cab. Any hopes that Robert Overton had that it would be well received were soon dashed. Geoff Trotter, managing director of the London General Cab Company and one of the biggest buyers of the FX3 said it was too big and too heavy. One proprietor, Barney Davis of Felday Cabs, strolled around it, took a draw on his trademark cigar and said, 'well, it's just a bloody awful vehicle, that's all I can say!' That evening, Robert Overton wrote in his diary, 'what a headache this is going to be!'

The prototype went on trial with York Way Motors in London's Kings Cross and the following November made its official debut at the Commercial Motor Show. It was priced at £1,198 and, like the FX3 and the pre-war Austin 12/4, was subsidised heavily by Austin. But when Carbodies tried to put it into production, the trouble started. Many of the press tools produced to build the body panels were so badly designed that many of those panels could not be made without major remedial work and over the course of the following year, just 150 cabs were delivered. This was a great embarrassment to Carbodies' parent company, BSA, who had announced in 1958 that they would be able to make at least fifty cabs a week. A lot of the equipment had to be redesigned and only by late 1959 were Carbodies able to begin delivery in quantity.

Photographed on a very misty day, this is the London General Cab Company's first Austin FX4. Those door handles would prove too flimsy for the rigours of London taxi work.

The Austin FX4, 1958-1968

Above: this 1959 example is possibly the oldest surviving FX4. The Austin badge on the grille was replaced with a simple script badge

Left: this circular aperture in the partition made communication very difficult and was soon replaced by a vertical, sliding glass panel

Below, left: darkened 'purdah' glass in the rear window gave some degree of privacy to the passengers, although with the amount of side glass, this was little more than a nod to old-fashioned practice

Below, right: brown leather seat facings and tan paint around the doors lasted until 1967.

From then on, the Austin FX4 began to take over from the FX3 as the most common cab on London's streets. At first, many Londoners let the new cabs go by, rather than hail them as they were unfamiliar with them, but they soon began to recognise the shape and they appreciated its comfortable ride. But drivers and proprietors thought that the FX4 was not a patch on the FX3. It was heavy to drive, it was draughty and it rattled and shook and when the gearbox, which was becoming very unreliable went wrong and when components began to break and metal met tortured metal, it gave out a scream like a banshee. There was no soundproofing fitted at all and after the engine had clocked up a lot of miles it became very noisy, making communication with the passengers difficult. Serious rust began to appear on the bodywork, with the bottoms of the doors falling out and the wings rotting at the seams. It was fortunate for Mann and Overton that they had such a hold on the market, because there was only one other cab available, the traditionally-styled Beardmore, whose factory could not produce anywhere the numbers the trade needed, even if the trade, including the fleet proprietors wanted them.

At first, only the diesel automatic version was available, but in 1961 Austin introduced a manual gearbox for the cab, which was adopted almost universally and in 1962 they also offered a petrol engine. This engine was also recommended by Austin for provincial taxi use, as they advised in the brochure that the diesel powered taxi ... 'is designed for urban operation over relatively flat terrain. It is strongly recommended therefore that, because of its increased performance, the petrol powered taxi with synchromesh gearbox is purchased if the vehicle is to be operated in hilly rural areas.' Now, with the manual box the FX4 was more reliable and it began to be accepted by the trade. It had to be: despite its shortcomings, there was nothing else that could compare with its serviceability and availability.

Alongside the Austin FX3 a hire car version, the FL1 had been made and it had a small but dedicated market. Many of its customers were hire car operators outside London, who found this vehicle an economical alternative to a Rolls-Royce or a Daimler. Other customers were funeral directors, who may also have bought hearses based on the FL1 chassis, and hospitals and nursing homes, who liked the access this type of vehicle gave. There were also some private buyers, who liked to have a vehicle that was as adept as a taxi in town traffic.

To keep this market, a hire car version of the FX4, the FL2 was also decided upon. Although basically the same vehicle, the FL2 had no for hire sign on the roof, a separate front passenger seat, its occasional seats faced forward and the moveable part of the partition glass slid from side to side, instead of up and down. Different too, was the clear glass in the back window. The petrol engine was a popular option, offering better performance for the hire car operator and the lower noise level provided some degree of discretion for funeral directors. Soon after the model's introduction, a higher-ratio differential was fitted, improving its top speed.

The Austin FL2 Hire Car, 1958-1967

Top: Although sharing the same body and mechanical specification as the taxi, the hire car carried no 'for hire' sign, had wing-mounted indicators and a rubbing strip along all four side panels. The Fairway Driver grille, indicator repeaters and stainless steel sill trims are non-original items on this preserved 1965 example

Above, left: the boot lid opens fully, restrained by steel straps; the number plate hinges down to be visible when the boot is open

Above, right: full-width glass in the partition slides horizontally. A fold-up seat is fitted in the front. This was popular with funeral directors as a place for a pallbearer to sit

Left: the FL2's two occasional seats folded out of the partition. Cord carpet was standard

Overseas sales, especially to America had been uppermost in the minds of Austin's sales department since the end of World War 2, and all their new, post-war models were designed to appeal to what they envisaged the Americans would want. Austin-Healey sports cars would prove a big hit, but the saloon cars were too flimsy and expensive to compete with big, robust and very cheap American cars. Attempts to sell the FX3 would also prove fruitless. Cost was a major factor in deterring the Americans, as well as the cab's driving position, which was upright and cramped compared to the big De Sotos and Checkers that American hack drivers were used to. Nor was it as economical or as powerful as the American cabs, and these attempts failed to secure a place for the cab in the USA.

A diesel FX4 of around 1960 vintage was exported to New York City lasting, remarkably until at least 1965, coping with that city's potholes and snowy winters. But in the face of cheap production cars, which the city had finally allowed in 1954 in place of specially-built limousine-type cars, nobody wanted this slow, noisy and expensive oddball.

In a speech in late 1967, the mayor of New York City, John V. Lindsay criticised these production car taxicabs, saying that they were unsuitable for the job because the tall, the elderly and infirm struggled to get in and out of them. Lindsay was six feet four inches tall, so he identified with these people. In the same speech he praised the FX4. He had also visited London's Commercial Motor Exhibition earlier that year and asked Carbodies' new director and general manager, Bill Lucas if he could buy a left-hand drive cab for use in his city. Lucas told him that no such version existed, but that didn't deter Austin from seizing an opportunity and on May 14 1968 at the Mayor's official residence, Gracie Mansion, Graham Whitehead, the president of British Motor Holdings (USA) Inc., (BMC's USA sales organisation) presented Mayor Lindsay with a specially built Austin FX4 for, as Whitehead himself put it, 'extended testing by the city'. The cab, which was basically a left-hand drive petrol FL2 was painted yellow, a colour that would be mandatory that year in New York City and fitted with an automatic gearbox. Also at the event was the vice-president of Peugeot France, Henri Combe, who presented a Peugeot 404 taxi. Both cabs were scheduled to run for six months,

This Austin FX4, photographed in New York City in 1965 is something of a mystery. Its door handles date it from around 1960, but it is left-hand drive and although it carries the for hire sign in the centre of the roof, mandatory in New York, there is no indication that a UK-type sign was ever fitted. This strongly suggests that it was specially built, but nobody can be found to say how it arrived in 'The Big Apple'

The special Austin sent to New York for evaluation in 1968, featuring heavy-duty bumpers, indicators mounted on the wings, centre-mounted 'for hire' sign and yellow paint

commencing on June 1 and there was talk of the possibility of licence-building whichever of the two came out best. The Austin drew the most favourable comments from the public, but against it was unbeatable competition from the domestic cars that New York operators were using. These cars came with power steering, automatic transmissions and power brakes and Ford, Chevrolet and Chrysler dealers outbid each other for shares in the market, all offering a 'taxi special' for around $2,750. Chrysler even offered 'baker's dozen' deals- buy twelve and get a thirteenth free.

Now in 1967, along came the Austin, priced at $3,500 with no power steering or power brakes, a draughty body that let in the worst that the North Atlantic winds could blow at it and a lack of acceleration that was nothing short of embarrassing. Even the safety glass partition, a highly promoted feature did not persuade potential buyers, who had already begun to install bullet-proof glass partitions in their own cabs. It was no surprise that it flopped.

Chapter 3
The 'New Shape'

Mann and Overton intended the FX4 to be in production for ten years and so in 1965, they began planning its replacement. They asked Carbodies for a price for a new cab body, and were quoted £35,000, which they turned down as too expensive. Mindful of the rust problem, they spoke to Jensen and to Gordon-Keeble, both of whom were making luxury sports cars with fibreglass bodies. A cab with a fibreglass body would obviate the rust problem, but Mann and Overton were warned off this material by Joe Edwards, the new managing director of BMC. The technology of fibreglass bodies was then comparatively new: it was difficult, if not impossible to achieve the superb finish available nowadays. Bearing out Edwards' warnings, problems were already occurring with the body and the paint finish of a new fibreglass-bodied taxi, the Winchester. And there would be concerns over maintenance. Cab repairers were geared up to fix steel cab bodies and if the new Austin were to have a fibreglass body, new men would have to be trained to use the new materials.

Quickly, Mann and Overton decided against fibreglass, and even against having a new body. Instead, they decided to have the FX4 revamped, putting right many of the complaints the trade had made over the previous decade and making it a better cab to ride in and to drive. Thanks to the arrival at Carbodies of a new director and general manager, Jim Munday and his technical and sales director, Bill Lucas, the build quality of the cab had been gradually improved, but apart from changing the seat facing material from leather to vinyl and the aforementioned addition of a manual gearbox and the replacement of the DG automatic gearbox, the specification had remained unchanged. Now, the FX4 would have a major revamp.

A Winchester Mk4. It was built for Winchester by Keewest Engineering, a company formed from Gordon-Keeble, the firm that quoted Mann and Overton for a fibreglass body. It is not beyond possibility that the Mk4 was based on a design produced originally by Gordon-Keeble for an Austin chassis, in other words, the original 'FX5'

The Austin FX4, 1968-1974

Top: as well as looking smarter, the 'new shape' FX4 was far better to drive than the original model The stainless steel sill trims date from 1971; solid rubber ones were fitted from late 1967

Above, left: the sliding glass of the FL2 was fitted to a raked-back partition

Above, right: the interior trim colour was changed to black and the floor mat to grey

Far left: the heater was fitted behind the driver's seat, with the outlets placed between the tip-up seats, greatly improving its effectiveness

Left: taillights came from the BMC's MkII 1100/1300

The addition of soundproofing reduced driver fatigue and, along with a new sliding partition improved communication between driver and passenger. A leak caused by rainwater collecting under the battery, which deposited water on the driver's right foot in wet weather was cured by altering the body panels under the bonnet. The passenger heater, virtually useless because the heater pipes ran under the chassis and were exposed to cold air was moved to the inside of the driver's compartment and the driver was given more legroom by raking back the partition. The appearance of the cab was altered by the fitting of new taillights with inbuilt indicators, doing away with the unloved roof-mounted ones. At long last, an internal rear view mirror was allowed, although it had to be placed on top of the dashboard, so as, in the age of the mini-skirt to reassure any young lady passengers that the driver was not trying to see anything he was not supposed to see!

Although it did not have an official designation, the trade called this latest model the 'new shape'. They approved of the changes, but they still expected a new cab sooner rather than later. However, what Mann and Overton were supplying was a vehicle the public had come to recognise as a taxi; some had doubts whether the modern-looking Mk4 Winchester, introduced at the same time was received in the same way, even though it was black, and its roof sign read 'taxi for hire'. But though the trade didn't particularly like the Mk4 Winchester, they did not criticise its styling for being too modern; in fact it was accepted as normal progress and they assumed that any forthcoming new Austin would also have modern styling.

The public's doubts about accepting London taxis with a modern look would be borne out by the experiences of those driving a new prototype, the Metrocab that appeared at the same time as the Mk4 Winchester. It was built by the bus, train and shipbuilders, Metro-Cammell-Weymann and, like the Winchester, it had a fibreglass-body. Just one prototype was tested, for two years with the London General Cab Company, who had the option to fund its production

The MCW Metrocab prototype from 1968, a smart, well-proportioned, modern-style vehicle whose appearance was not recognised by everyone as what a taxi should look like

and to act as dealers. But few drivers wanted to take it out, even though it was available at a lower rent, because they claimed the public did not recognise it as a taxi and they were losing work as a result. Faced with this situation, and the reality of having to bring in men skilled in the repair of fibreglass bodies the General opted to keep their FX4s, a vehicle their drivers had come to accept, if not love and one the public recognised.

As a means of contributing to a cleaner environment, and as an attempt to reduce running costs, west London cab fleet owners W. H. Cook and Sons bought a fleet of petrol FX4s and converted them to run on liquid propane gas (LPG), as there was no fuel duty on it at the time and thus was considerably cheaper. Although the petrol FX4 returned about 18mpg, compared to the 25mpg-plus of the diesel, the absence of fuel duty on LPG reduced the fuel costs by about one-third. At first, the project went well, despite some minor technical problems but it turned sour in early 1971 when the government announced its intention to put duty on LPG. W. H. Cook's managing director Vernon Cook wrote to Parliament, saying, 'we regret that any excessive excise duty would kill off the project and with it the end of hopes for a cleaner city.' Cook would be disappointed, as tax was levied on LPG and killed off the advantages of the gas cab.

Although the trade bought the new version in record numbers, many members of the trade wanted nothing less that a totally new cab. With the collapse of the Metrocab project and the demise of the poor-selling Winchester in 1972, Mann and Overton found themselves by default in a monopoly situation. There was a campaign in 'Taxi', the magazine of the Licensed Taxi Drivers Association, demanding that the PCO change the Conditions of Fitness, to allow more makers into the market and also bring the price of a cab, now around £1200, down. But it was not a situation that Mann and Overton had deliberately created. The fact was that almost nobody else thought that making a London cab was a worthwhile job, and nobody but Mann and Overton were committed to the trade to the same extent.

During the early 1970s, several changes, both to the specification of the cab and to Carbodies, locked the FX4 into another decade of production. BMC had supplied the chassis from the start, at first from the Austin factory at Longbridge but from 1960 from their massive Adderley Park, Birmingham factory. By early 1970, it was Adderley Park's only product and British Leyland, within whom BMC was now amalgamated decided to close the factory and the chassis manufacturing equipment was transferred to Carbodies in early 1971. Later that year a bigger, 2.5-litre diesel engine was fitted to the cab, which gave it better pulling power, enabling it to cope better with an automatic gearbox and from then on, the automatic box started to become more popular, making the cab less arduous to drive in London traffic.

The Austin FX4, 1974-1982

Above: plastic overriders appeared in 1977

Right: in 1974, the Austin FX4 was modified to comply with European safety regulations. modifications included opening quarterlights, push-button door handles and burstproof locks

Below, left to right: interior door handles were moved to the centre of the door, the instrument panel was redesigned and column self-cancelling indicator switch, new steering wheel with protective centre and steering column lock were fitted and the rear seat cushion was re-profiled

Unreported by the cab trade press, however was the story that Carbodies' owner, BSA had turned in a loss of over £3m in 1971. Since the mid-1960s, most of their income had come from making motorcycles, sales of which had been severely hit by cheap and much more reliable Japanese imports. Prompted by the government, Manganese Bronze Holdings, (MBH) who owned Norton Motorcycles, bought BSA. At the time, they had no idea that they had also bought a company that made London taxis but, thankfully, the importance of the cab was immediately recognised and Carbodies were more or less left alone to make it. But industrial strife within MBH's motorcycle interests would drain the group of funds and this, coupled with the financial problems that were emerging within Austin's parent company, British Leyland ensured that there would be no money forthcoming for a new Austin cab for some time.

However, money would be needed to upgrade the cab to meet new regulations, brought into effect when Britain joined the EEC in January 1973. Burst-proof door locks, crash-proof steering and a new dashboard and steering wheel were fitted to comply with the regulations, and the revised model was introduced in the spring of 1974. A downside of the regulations was that the FX4's optional petrol engine would not comply with new exhaust emission regulations. As the FX4 and FL2 were now the only vehicle fitted with this engine, British Leyland scrapped it rather than try and modify it.

Since the FX4's introduction, two optional colours, white and carmine red had been offered besides the standard black. From 1973, a range of new colours was offered, including aconite, (a bright shade of purple) grass green, brown and blackcurrant. They were not popular, the fleet proprietors preferring black, as they had only to keep one colour in stock in the body shop. Besides, they knew full well that a different colour cab, which cost more, earned exactly the same money as a black one!

Carbodies' managing director, Bill Lucas had been discontented with his relationship with Mann and Overton for some time. The dealers were set on keeping the FX4 in production, despite the increasing demand for a new model, and they would not pass on complaints about the cab they thought were insignificant. Carbodies, who had made a wide range of vehicles in their history now only made the FX4 and Lucas felt that the market for a new, modern model would be substantial, especially outside London. Thus he set in motion the FX5 project, which he would finance, independent of Mann and Overton and thus free of their constraints.

There were other pressures on him too. Carbodies had always had other sources of work from the motor industry, but these were now rapidly drying up, as manufacturers decided it was more economical to make additional bodies such as estate cars 'in-house'. The last car to be subcontracted to Carbodies, the Triumph 2000 estate car was due for deletion in 1977. Jake Donaldson, Carbodies' engineering director had for some time considered that the roof of the

A scale model of the FX5, a modern-style cab that was to be produced by Carbodies

Range Rover would suit a cab body, and based his initial designs for the FX5 on it, but it soon became clear that it was unsuitable and so he went ahead with a completely new design. It would have a new, as yet untried Peugeot engine, a new chassis with running gear from the all-new Rover SD1 and a completely new, modern-style body. A scale model was built and presented to the board of MBH and the go-ahead was given to build it.

But bad news was on the horizon: the troubled British Leyland had been nationalised and as the 1970s drew to a close, its new boss, Michael Edwardes set in motion a major plan of rationalisation, prior to it being sold back to private owners. Part of the plan involved selling off the cab's diesel engine to India, leaving the 2.2-litre Land Rover as BL's only in-house diesel. Lucas was warned that this engine was totally unsuitable for the cab, and so opted for Peugeot engine he had planned to use in the FX5. Fitted into an existing model it was tested in Birmingham and for the most part appeared to run satisfactorily, so the decision was taken that the Peugeot engine would power the FX4 when it was ready. Unfortunately, Bill Lucas had been in poor health, and in February 1979 he took early retirement. His plans for the Peugeot engine and for the FX5 now hung in the balance.

Carbodies' engineering director and designer of the FX4, Jake Donaldson, (far right) and Bill Lucas, Carbodies' managing director (centre right) chat to HRH the Prince of Wales at Buckingham Palace. The occasion was a London cab trade visit in 1977 to commemorate HM Queen Elizabeth II's Silver Jubilee

Chapter 4
Carbodies Takes Over

Carbodies' new managing director, Grant Lockhart, knew full well he needed to increase taxi production to make the factory viable. A change in the finance laws brought in lease-purchase, which opened up to potential new owner-drivers the chance to buy a new cab with a deposit equivalent to just one month's hire purchase payment. This ought to have increased sales, but in fact only helped cushion what would otherwise have been a dramatic drop during the 'Winter of Discontent' and its aftermath, a period at the end of the 1970s that would slow the nation's economy and with it the cab trade's earning power.

A new optional colour, midnight blue was added to the original red and white. It became a popular choice, offering something different but still discreet. Along with other extra-cost options such as vinyl roofs and sun roofs these colours would increase Mann and Overton's profit margins without any major capital investment. The new owner-drivers, so long used to the standard black of their rented cabs bought different colour cabs in the their dozens, often specifying the newly named HL or HLS models that had vinyl roofs, tilting sun roofs, reversing lights and rear and front fog lights included.

Another new law, soon to come into force demanded that all passenger-carrying vehicles should comply with National Type Approval regulations and be tested as part of the approval process. BL, as British Leyland had now been renamed were loath to lay out the money needed to bring the cab into compliance when it was struggling to put in place the complete reconstruction of the organisation so vital for its very existence. The only option open was for Carbodies to acquire the intellectual rights to the FX4 and get it type-approved in their own name. Now, the cab would not receive the already-diminishing subsidy it had enjoyed from Austin, and Carbodies had to put the price up by £1,000 to £8,000. In the spring of 1982, what was the Austin FX4 became the Carbodies FX4, identical in every respect except for the name on the badges.

The Peugeot diesel on test in the FX4 was proving to be unreliable, so it was scrapped and in its place went the Land Rover engine, mated to a 5-speed Rover manual gearbox and the Borg Warner automatic from the FX4. There was also a petrol version of the engine available, and this too was offered, with the same choice of transmissions. Carried over were the three trim

FX4R TAXI

Engineered and Purpose-Built – To Last!

By Carbodies Of Coventry – Taxi Makers to the World.

The Carbodies FX4R

Top: 'purpose-built' was true of the FX4R: 'Taxi Makers to the World' was a hope that was not fulfilled until the end of the 1980s. 'Built to last' was less than accurate with regard to the model: very few survive today in comparison with other versions
Right: Carbodies' logo was designed by engineer Derek Cripps, who would be head-hunted by MCW for work on the Metrocab
Below, left: further ventures into the American market had to wait for the London Coach and London Sterling episode
Below, right: only the 'Carbodies' badges on the boot lid and grille distinguished the FX4R from the previous model

Austin FX4Q

Top: the FX4Q Rebuilt Taxi is distinguishable from the FX4R by its Austin badge

Above, left: floor change for the automatic gearbox and pendant pedals were new for the 'R' and the 'Q'. Red light on the lower right of the instrument panel indicates the operation of the motion door locks. A new steering wheel boss badge covered the obsolete Leyland symbol

Above, right: interior remained unchanged from the Austin

Right: rear fog light and reversing light were optional extras. Heated rear window was standard from 1978

options; FL, HL and HLS and the full range of colours. The new model was named the FX4R and it had many new features that were long overdue, including optional power steering and full-servo brakes as well as a new colour option, Rattan Beige. With its extra equipment, and with Carbodies no longer enjoying financial support from Austin the FX4R was bound to be more expensive: prices started at £8,869 for the basic FL manual without no power steering, to £10,072 for an HLS automatic with power steering as standard.

With a petrol engine once more available, Grant Lockhart also saw an opportunity to revive the FL2, and re-market it as 'The London Limousine', with the option of a leather interior and any other luxury item the customer desired. 'A Luxury executive limousine in a class of its own, styled to your personal taste', said its brochure.

The FX4R's top speed was higher and it was much quieter, but unfortunately its acceleration and pulling power were hopeless and so was its fuel consumption. The engine was prone to overheating and would go out of tune very quickly. Thanks to the fitting of wrongly recommended components, the manual gearbox and clutch would self-destruct, often within the first year. Sales came crashing down, even as the demand for cabs was increasing: unemployment was growing and more and more men undertook the Knowledge of London, the strict test every aspiring London cab driver has to undergo. The Public Carriage Office had no option but to allow older Austin FX4s to be licensed beyond the ten-year age limit, just to make sure there were enough cabs on the road.

The failure of the Land Rover engine gave an opportunity to specialists to offer modifications to the engine and also different engines for those prepared to pay for them. Most popular was the fitting of a stronger timing chain to the Land Rover, which improved its reliability and fuel consumption by keeping it in tune. The London Cab Company (formerly the London General) offered a conversion of the engine to 2.5 litres, but the most popular conversion choice was the 3-litre Perkins engine by Motor & Diesel of Cambridgeshire. A 3.5 litre

Based on a Range Rover body, the CR6 was to be the London taxi of the 1980s. To make it look different from the Range Rover, the grille and lights from a Morris Ital were fitted

Mazda was even more powerful but there were few takers for it. The London Cab Company fitted a Ford FSD diesel, as used in the Transit, but it was noisy and it is beleived that no more than two prototypes were built. Carbodies themselves made a one-off petrol automatic FX4R with a Laycock deNormanville overdrive, finished in Rattan Beige, which is now in preservation. Another FX4R was fitted with a 2-litre ohc 4-cylinder Austin engine. However, high fuel consumption meant that few petrol cabs were sold.

Grant Lockhart considered that the FX5 would be too expensive to produce and he scrapped it, but he knew that a new model was essential and, using his connections within the BL combine began work on a new cab based on a Range Rover body. It would be called the CR6. However, it would be doomed almost from the start by a project that ironically would be the future salvation of the company- wheelchair accessibility for taxis. In 1980, as part of the International Year of the Disabled, the Department of Transport discovered that the majority of wheelchair users wanted access to taxis, as the state of the pavements was so bad they often couldn't get to bus stops, even if they could get on the buses in the first place. The civil servant in charge of the project, Ann Frye asked Carbodies if a taxi could accept a wheelchair. In theory it could: the doors opened wide enough, but the angled partition introduced in 1968 narrowed the accessible width to a point where access was difficult, if not impossible. But a wheelchair fitted in the CR6, so two prototypes were put on trial as wheelchair-carrying vehicles outside of London. This delayed the introduction of the model until at least 1985, and with cab sales at a record low, the company was in trouble.

It would be entirely wrong to say that no cabs left the factory in the three years the FX4R was in production. A significant number were sold to new cab drivers, who had experienced how heavy the steering and brakes were on older cabs and would forgo the slow acceleration for more creature comforts. Also, the FX4R's power steering and servo brakes meant a gradual increase in the number of women cab drivers in London. Previously, if they had completed the Knowledge of London, they found the existing Austin cabs (which is what would be supplied to them as new drivers who had yet to establish any safety or reliability record to justify giving them a new vehicle) far too heavy to drive and did not stay in the trade. The older hands, meantime held on to their Austins and weathered the storm, seeing the value of them rise as the second-hand value of FX4Rs slumped. The reduction of new cabs licensed and the demand from owners of older cabs to keep them running forced the PCO to abolish their unwritten rule of only allowing cabs to be licensed for ten years. Now, with more and more cab drivers and fewer new cabs, it was vital to allow the older models to remain in service.

To keep Carbodies' production lines moving, Grant Lockhart sanctioned the development of a competitor for the FX4R, the FX4Q. Old FX4 chassis were stripped and overhauled by a company called Rebuilt Taxicabs Ltd of Hackney, east London. The chassis then went to Carbodies' factory, where they were fitted with a complete new body and an Indian-made diesel engine identical to the Austin engine that BL had sold a couple of years before. The model was called the FX4Q, because Department of Transport legislation demanded that all examples were given the non year-related index number suffix 'Q', as the actual age of the cab could not be established.

It was Lockhart's intention to sell at least as many cabs in the provincial market as were sold in London. Carbodies Sales and Service had been set up in 1976 when Austin decided they no longer wanted to sell cabs directly to the provinces. This company would serve new dealerships around the country. They could not have picked a worse vehicle than the FX4R with which to do this. Its unreliability, as well as a poorly established, and in some places virtually non-existent parts supply network gave Carbodies and the FX4 in general a reputation that would be difficult, and in some quarters impossible to live down.

Carbodies' difficulties caused Mann and Overton great concern and, feeling that their supplier might go out of business, they decided they should look for a completely new supplier for a cab. They had the financial backing: in 1977, they had been taken over by Lloyd's and Scottish, the people who had underwritten their financial services since 1936. They commissioned a chassis from Robert Jankel, the proprietor of the Panther Westwinds Car Company, but although a chassis was made, with a 2.3 litre Ford diesel and disc brakes, there would be some major changes at Carbodies and the project was scrapped.

America offered a lifeline. An attempt in the 1970s to get smaller cabs, including the FX4 into New York had ended as unsuccessfully as that of 1968, as Carbodies could not meet the

An FX4R on the rank at London's Victoria Station. Speaking to the driver is the late Harry Feigen, then General Secretary of the Licensed Taxi Drivers Association and later, the first Master of the Worshipful Company of Hackney Carriage Drivers

The London Coach and London Sterling

Detail differences such as no 'for hire' sign, lights and bumpers distinguish the London Coach from its British counterpart. This preserved example is finished in British Racing Green. Other colours available were International Yellow, Black, Carmine Red, Rattan Beige and Midnight Blue. The Sterling limousine version was offered with optional silver or Midnight Blue metallic overspray

Below, left and right: London Coach Inc fitted the cab out with this very smart interior, available in vinyl (shown here) or velour. Colours were charcoal grey (illustrated), British Tan and Deep Blue

demand for orders of 2,000 or more, but in 1984, when they were totally dependent on the FX4, the chance of not only selling, but having cabs licence-built in the USA was one they grasped eagerly. Grant Lockhart's long-standing connections with Ford in the USA, put him in touch with a specialist motor manufacturer, D. F. Landers in Mount Clemens, Michigan. Landers was an ex-serviceman whose business was manufacturing specialist vehicles for military applications. Landers set up the London Coach Company Inc., where he would to adapt the cab to suit the US market and and build it and sell it both in taxi and limousine form. The taxi would be called 'The London Coach' and the limousine, the 'The London Sterling', which was marketed as a compact, highly manouvrable alternative to the monstrous stretch limousines that could be seen on every US city street. The plan was to make and sell around 500 vehicles in three years, with Carbodies supplying the bodies in completely knocked down (CKD) form, i. e. a complete set of body panels and chassis, that Landers would assemble in his own factory.

The FX4R's Land Rover petrol engine did not comply with the US Federal Government's tough emission regulations, so the engine Landers would use was a US-made 2.3 litre four cylinder Ford Pinto, with a 3-speed automatic transmission. Ford saw this as superb publicity and co-operated fully, ensuring the engine complied with the US emission regulations. The Ford was a powerful engine, and Grant Lockhart recalled being stopped for speeding by the Highway Patrol on the interstate freeway. He didn't get a ticket; the cops couldn't stop laughing at the idea of a London taxi being stopped for speeding at 85mph!

Landers produced the cab well, with a special interior. Missing was the roof-mounted 'taxi' sign, as US operators preferred, or were obliged to use the centrally-placed sign incorporating the 'hired/free' lights. The London Limousine offered leather trim, a cocktail cabinet with Brierley crystal glasses, cellular phone and in-car entertainment in the form of a stereo cassette player and colour TV. Both models attracted a lot of interest, but sales were soon to be crippled by an exchange rate of around 2.5 dollars to the pound, which inflated the price of the cab to well over the $17,000 Landers had planned, whereas the most popular US taxis, the Ford LTD and the Chevrolet Caprice, cost around $11,000. By mutual agreement the project was scrapped, with about fifty vehicles already delivered and another 150 in the pipeline.

Chapter 5
London Taxis International

It was clear that Carbodies had to make improvements to the FX4R, both for the sake of the London cab trade and for their own survival. They needed the income from sales in London, which had slumped and also to have better product for the provincial market, in order to increase their production. A new managing director, Barry Widdowson put in place the production changes needed to improve the build quality of the cab and he ordered the installation of the new 2.5 litre Land Rover engine, coupled to a Borg Warner BW40 automatic gearbox or the 5-speed manual of the FX4R. Gone was the petrol engine option for the cab and the London Limousine as a separate model line was abandoned. The new cab, launched on November 4 1985 was named the FX4S. New switchgear was fitted on the dashboard, because Lucas had ceased manufacture of the old types, which had been used since 1958. Some of the draughts that had chilled a generation of cab drivers were, to some extent tamed by the fitting of new plastic sill cappings and new also were rolled steel bumpers, finished in matt black. These were fitted because the old tools that had made the cab bumpers since its introduction had worn out, and Carbodies were not prepared to pay out a considerable amount of money for new tools to make the old type bumpers. On the road prices of the FX4S started at £11,239 for the basic manual model, almost £2,500 more than the equivalent FX4R. Slightly easier to bear was the price of the HLS, which at £11,737 was an increase of £2,140. Despite improvements to the build quality, problems arose with a batch of cam belts, which were prone to breakage. The overheating problem persisted too, despite Carbodies' insistence that it didn't.

The black bumpers fitted to the FX4S were made, initially as an interim, economy measure because it was only supposed to be in production until the CR6 was introduced, but on releasing the FX4S in November 1985 at their new premises in Carnwath Road, Fulham, Mann and Overton announced, 'we believe that with the FX4S we have a vehicle that would see us well into the twenty-first century'. The dismay the trade felt when they read this was palpable, because it implied that the CR6 was dead and that they would be condemned to drive was a virtual relic for another two decades. That would prove to be true, and was confirmed by an announcement, three months later, in January 1986, when an MBH press release claimed that the traditional style cab was what the trade now wanted, but in truth the CR6 was simply too big a job for Carbodies to pull off on their own, with the finances and expertise they had to hand.

32

But it would be a move from an unexpected quarter that would end Mann and Overton's overall control of the cabs they had sponsored over the decades, and improve the vehicle beyond any reasonable expectation. In 1985, Lloyd's and Scottish, who had owned Mann and Overton since 1976 put the dealership up for sale and Manganese Bronze bought it. Now, everything was under one roof and there would be no more wrangling about whether such and such a modification would be funded: if it was worth doing, it would be done, with the decision to do so made internally. With the purchase, MBH formed a new company, London Taxis International, with three divisions: LTI Carbodies, who would make cabs; LTI Mann and Overton, who would sell them and LTF, London Taxi Finance, who would help both owner-drivers and fleet proprietors to buy them. The FX4S would be the first cab to carry the LTI logo.

But the bitter truth facing LTI was that they could not survive for too long with a vehicle as antiquated as the FX4S. The London market was too small to support the factory and many of the provinces, where they had a choice of vehicles didn't want it. But now there was a rival, the Metrocab. Introduced in the spring of 1987, it was made by Metro-Cammell-Weymann, the company that had produced a prototype some twenty years before. The Metrocab was revolution compared to the FX4S. It was modern in appearance, it was draught-free, its fibreglass body was rust-free, it could seat five passengers where the PCO would only license the FX4S for four and, most importantly, it was wheelchair accessible. New regulations would come into place by January 1989 demanding that all purpose-built cabs had this facility. At one point in the summer of 1987, the number of Metrocabs licensed by the PCO exceeded that of the FX4S. It seemed that only a new cab from LTI could turn things around, but a new cab was something they couldn't yet produce. 'Yet' was the operative word. LTI's new engineering director, Ed Osmond began work on a new design of cab, developing the running gear bit by bit, taking what he called, 'bite-sized chunks' and fitting each major improvement to successive new versions of the FX4, so as to both improve the old cab and have it right for the

The MCW Metrocab's introduction gave great cause for concern at LTI. The cab's unreliable automatic gearbox and the collapse of MCW, which caused a hiatus in Metrocab sales gave LTI some breathing space

next generation. But first, LTI had to improve the FX4S still further, to generate new provincial sales as well as recoup market share from Metrocab in London. They recruited a new man, Jevon Thorpe to redesign the interior to make it better, front and rear than the Metrocab. They also needed a new engine, and engaged engine specialists Ricardo Engineering to find one. Ricardo located what they considered the best of its type at Nissan in Japan, but it did not come with suitable transmissions, which was what LTI needed to avoid repeating the fiasco of the FX4R. If they could wait a year, they were told, a much better powertrain would be available. They would wait, and would also wait to install wheelchair accessibility.

The next model would be an upgrade of the FX4S, the FX4S-Plus, with an all-new, five-seat interior, in grey vinyl, and a new dashboard and trim for the driver. The engine would be the 2.5 Litre Land Rover diesel from the FX4S. There were two new colours, City Grey and Royal Burgundy. The S-Plus received a warm reception on its launch in November 1987 and soon put LTI back on top.

But there would be something very special soon, a real swansong for the FX4, the Fairway. It was, without a doubt the best version of the FX4 ever made, a fitting finale after three decades of production. It served two purposes: one, it gave LTI a credible vehicle with which to re-enter UK markets and try previously-untapped overseas markets and two, it provided a rolling test-bed for the new running gear that would be used in the next generation of taxi.

To power it, LTI bought in what was unquestionably the best engine ever installed in an FX4, the Nissan TD27 2.7 litre diesel. It was smooth, quiet, economical and above all, proved to be almost unbelievably reliable and long-lived. Mileages of almost half a million were not unknown by the time some of the earliest examples came off the road in the mid-2000s. The transmissions too were almost bombproof, with the four-speed automatic standing anything

Conversions for wheelchair accessibility were pioneered at Carbodies Sales & Services premises at Tollington Avenue, Coventry. Here are six converted cabs, mostly FX4S models destined for a provincial operator

The LTI FX4S-Plus

Above: the FX4S-Plus inherited its black bumpers and silver wheels from the FX4S. An additional badge bearing the word "Plus' was fitted to the grille and the boot lid

Right: the 'Plus' had a larger radiator with inbuilt cooler for the BW40 automatic gearbox. Brake servo and pendant pedals were carried over from the FX4R and FX4S

Below: the most important differences were inside, including a new, grey vinyl dash and steering wheel, (left) and grey interior, which could seat five. Vinyl trim (illustrated) was standard, velour was optional

that a working cab driver in the toughest of urban driving conditions could throw at it. The five-speed manual gearbox was robust and slick, an ideal choice for the provincial operator who, where the London man always chose an automatic, much preferred the manual option. Most importantly, the cab had full wheelchair accessibility, with the rear seat designed to tip up to allow the wheelchair to fit in the recess in the new dogleg partition.

The interior trim was carried over from the FX4S-Plus, as was the dashboard, but a new style sunroof, sliding instead of tilting was fitted as standard on the top of the range 'Gold' model. The Gold also featured headrests and wood veneer door cappings. The lower range models, the 'Silver' and 'Bronze' were less luxuriously trimmed, but still were of the same mechanical specification. The colours offered in addition to black included Midnight Blue, Cardinal Red, (close to, but brighter than the old Carmine red) City Grey, Sherwood Green, Rattan Beige and Royal Burgundy. The cab was introduced in February 1989 and its welcome was beyond that given to any previous model. Prices started at £14,273.80 for the Bronze manual to £16,749.75 for the Gold Automatic. Sales of over 3000 for the following full year broke all records.

Wheelchair accessibility was now a major selling point, and would be the key that would open the door to the provincial markets. But the local authorities, which license hackney carriages outside of London needed persuading that such a feature was necessary in their areas, and that London-type cabs were the best vehicles to provide it. Some authorities, such as Birmingham, Manchester and Glasgow accepted this with little argument, as they only permitted the use of London-type cabs. However, many provincial operators, like some London proprietors balked at having to pay a premium for wheelchair accessibility when they felt they would get little or no work from it, and indeed some objected most strongly to having what they saw as vehicles that were totally unsuitable for their terrain foisted upon them, with some even resorting to action in the courts. However, LTI won through in many cases and put the Fairway

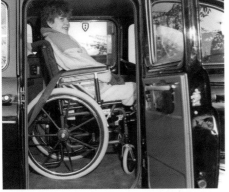

onto provincial roads where London cabs had never been seen before. Often, to satisfy the local trade the licensing authority would allow a mixed fleet of saloon cars and

How a passenger in a wheelchair is safely carried, secured in a rearward-facing position, according to the Transport Road Research Laboratory. Note also how the door opens clear of the aperture on its swan-neck hinges

The LTI Fairway

Above: the Fairway had a different grille from the S-Plus, larger glass in the windscreen (although the aperture was identical, the rubber was slimmer) and red strips in the bumper rubbers

Right, upper: partition aperture was directly behind the driver. Passenger heater controls were moved to the partition and the fare table to the offside door

Right, lower: 'Fairway' script on the left hand side of the bootlid identifies the model from behind. An additional badge on the right marks the different 'Gold', Silver' and Bronze versions

Below, left: swan-neck hinges allow both rear doors to open without obstructing the door aperture

Below, right: moulded plastic door handles replaced the chromed items of the S-Plus

The LTI Fairway Driver

Above: domed hubcaps identify the 'Driver' from the earlier Fairway

Left: an opening window in the left hand side of the partition was fitted to all later Fairway Drivers. The red button on the left hand side, above the seat controls the wheelchair securing strap

Below, left: on the Driver 95, one half of the split rear seat lifts to allow extra legroom for a wheelchair user whilst the other half remains lowered to give space for a seated passenger

Below, centre: swivel seat and low step are aids to the infirm

Below, right: pairs of wheelchair ramps are provided with every Fairway and Fairway Driver. Red grab handles and seat fronts are aids for the visually-impaired

The Austin FX4's stylist, Eric Bailey, (standing) poses with Andrew Overton, grandson of Mann and Overton's founder, Tom Overton with the newly introduced Fairway Driver

London cabs, a compromise between local preference and the requirement to meet the needs of those in wheelchairs.

There was more work to be done on the cab itself. With the exception of the full servo, the brakes were little different from those of the 1958 model and the suspension was still the same. Disc brakes were now a necessity in modern traffic, especially on dual carriageways and motorways. LTI recruited specialists AP Lockheed to develop new brakes, including discs with four-pot callipers on the front, and went to GKN for a completely new front suspension that would accommodate the huge brakes, and a new back axle. These were fitted into the last version of the FX4, the Fairway Driver, announced in February 1992.

Disabled passengers appreciated two innovations on the Fairway Driver. One was a low step, which could be slipped into special mountings under the nearside passenger door and allowed easier access when there was no kerb nearby. The step was also designed for use with a swivel seat. The tip-up seat on the nearside could swivel out at an angle and be locked into place so that those who had difficulty in bending down to get into the cab could sit on the seat and be swung around into the cab. Disappointing for LTI was that sales slumped, not because of the taxi, the new features of which were welcomed, but because the country went into recession and, following the Gulf War American tourists, a mainstay of the trade stopped coming to London. Work levels plummeted in the worst period the London cab trade had experienced since the early 1950s and cab proprietors hung on to what they had until the work improved. As work improved, a rise in sales from 1995, confirmed the trade's approval of the 'Driver'.

Further modifications were fitted to the Fairway Driver Plus, including a new hatch in the partition that allowed passenger to pay from within the cab. This was found to be very unpopular, as it created a draught around the driver's neck. The Fairway 95, introduced, appropriately enough in 1995 featured a split rear seat. Half of this seat could remain in an elevated position to allow a slightly larger wheelchair to be carried but still have a passenger

The LTI TX1 was clearly and deliberately styled to look like a modern version of the FX4. Pictured is the 'Quartz Gold' special edition model

seated on the other half of the rear seat. New, patterned material was used to cover the seats, which also had a red front edge to make them more visible to the partially sighted. Weweler air suspension was offered on the rear axle as an optional extra, although the takeup was low.

From late 1995, work began in earnest on the new model, the TX1, and it was released in October 1997. The chairman of MBH, Jamie Borwick announced the new model in 'The Steering Wheel' trade paper and offered all who had ordered Fairway Drivers the chance to cancel and wait for a TX1. Most declined. Production of the Fairway Driver ceased in October 1997 and the very last one off the production line was sent to the National Motor Museum in Beaulieu, Hampshire. It carried the registration number 'R1 PFX' or, put another way, 'RIP FX'.

But that was not the end. Many Austin FX4s continued working in London until 1999 and beyond: new rules laid down by the Disability Discrimination Act demanded all cabs in London had to be wheelchair-accessible, and many older cabs were converted. Further regulations, this time put in place by Transport for London, a part of newly formed Greater London Authority, which was now in charge of the PCO called for all cabs to comply with new Euro 3 exhaust emission standards. The Fairway only complied with Euro 2, so rather than take their old Fairways off the road, many proprietors chose to spend up to £2,000 on conversions that were offered to make the Nissan engine compliant, rather than upgrade to new or secondhand examples of the then current LTI TXII, which was proving expensively unreliable. Remarkable was the fact that a single FX4R and two FX4S-Pluses, converted to Nissan power were still operating at the beginning of 2009.

Chapter 6
The FX4 Around the World

The name 'London Taxis International' was not selected by LTI's owner, Manganese Bronze Holdings Plc without good reason: the company wanted, indeed needed to expand into overseas markets to ensure its survival and future prosperity. From the days of the FX3, sales of taxis in London had been Mann and Overton's prerogative by contract. After all, they had sponsored Austin cabs from the late 1920s and had a right to this. But outside of London, with the exception of Manchester, where M & O had a dealership, sales were Austin's responsibility. But by 1976, Austin had become part of British Leyland and in their severe financial state decided not to continue selling the FX4. Compounding the difficulty was a new act that enabled local authorities to license private hire (minicabs). One clause forbade the use of any vehicle approved by the PCO as a taxi for private hire. This effectively killed off the FL2 as a provincial hire car and with it a small but significant percentage of Carbodies' production. To fill the gap, in the sales outlet at least Carbodies formed a subsidiary company, Carbodies Sales and Service, based at Tollington Avenue in Coventry.

In September 1983 Grant Lockhart, who had been Carbodies' managing director was moved to Carbodies Sales and Service, whilst Barry Widdowson took his place at Carbodies. When Lockhart had taken over at Carbodies, the taxi was the only product the company made. He tried to set up new model lines, as the company had done for most of its existence. These included a convertible version of the Mk4 Ford Cortina and a truck version of the Range Rover, the Unitruck, but these had failed and now the company's viability- indeed its very survival depended on sales of the taxi and the revived FL2, which was marketed as the London Limousine. Provincial sales, which had always been small by comparison to London but very important were one outlet, but export markets were entered into as well. A left-hand drive version of the current model, the FX4R was engineered and it was hoped that the new power steering, power brakes and optional five speed gearbox with a much lighter diaphragm clutch would be enough of an attraction. Unfortunately, the rest of the package was well below standard and the cab would fail even more dramatically overseas than it had done at home.

The first overseas markets tackled were in the Middle East with Kuwait, where most vehicles delivered were limousines; Saudi Arabia, where all the taxis were painted yellow to emulate US practice; Sharjah, in the United Arab Emirates, where a black taxi was delivered and to Quatar. All were supplied with petrol engines. The exercise was a disaster almost from the start. The air conditioning could not cope with the very high temperatures of the region and the engine proved unsuitable. Nor were the customers prepared to undertake the level of servicing required and sadly, Carbodies Sales and Service could not provide sufficient after-sales back-up to its customers. Within two years the project was abandoned. Other individual sales went to Japan and Turkey and attempts in the US with a mildly-modified cab did not succeed. When the FX4S was introduced in 1985, the left-hand drive package was abandoned, and ambitions for overseas sales, shelved.

The introduction of the Fairway, a far superior vehicle in every way to its predecessors and the product of London Taxis International, marked a return to overseas markets and this time the success was significant. For LTI, a most satisfying sales market must have been Germany, in the heart of Mercedes-Benz territory, with many cabs sold there. One of its principal attractions was driver safety. An increasing number of German taxi drivers had been the victims of armed robbery and the partition offered an extra line of defence. Also the motion locks prevented passengers from running off without paying. Germany has special taxi service centres and here LTI provided the kind of parts back-up and

Top: a yellow FX4R destined for Saudi Arabia, pictured beside one of the CR6 prototypes
Centre: a German Fairway Driver
Bottom: this Fairway Driver was one of a number sold to Portugal. Others, painted white went to Spain

One of the original Fairways
sold to the Tibs transport
company of Singapore

servicing expertise demanded. Other European taxi sales included Portugal, Denmark, Switzerland, and also 300 with Rover petrol engines were sold to Kenya.

The Far East provided other markets, but not for the first time. Limousine versions had been imported into Japan in the 1970s as part of an exchange deal involving Japanese-made firearms, but in the 1990s, Singapore bus and taxi operator Tibs bought 100 Fairway taxis, which proved to be a popular choice for clients of Singapore's wedding halls, not only because they are distinctive vehicles but because by tradition, a bride's outfit has a long, straight skirt and it is easier for her to get in and out of a London taxi than a saloon car. Fairway limousines were sold to the world-Famous Raffles Hotel in Singapore, but that city was the only Far Eastern market that took taxi versions. All other Far Eastern markets took limousines, including Japan, Hong Kong and Taiwan. Japanese taxis use LPG by law and there was no production version of the Fairway with a suitable engine, so all sales were of Fairway limousines, which were used by company directors for use as mobile offices; it is understood that the chairman of Sony had one. LTI supplied the vehicles fitted with air conditioning, leather seats and carpets and Nissan, who were acting directly on LTI's behalf fitted them with, telephones, fax, and telex. (These were the days before the internet) These items were essential because the directors would travel for up to 6 hours a day in Japan's extremely congested traffic. In some vehicles a massager was built into the driver's and passengers' seats to ease backache when sitting for so long!

This City Grey Fairway was one of
300 with Rover petrol engines sold
to Kenya

43

This very smart limousine, based on a Fairway Driver was supplied to a private owner in Taiwan

Before selling to overseas markets, be they to fleet operators or individuals, LTI insist upon full service facilities being in place before the deal goes ahead. To do otherwise would be to setting themselves up for trouble.

And it's not only new FX4s that got exported. Examples of such an iconic vehicle are in demand all around the world today, as far afield as the USA and Australia even after having travelled almost half a million miles at work. Owners have formed themselves into local clubs, and one of the most active clubs is Crazy Cabs of Paris. The club began in 1980 when a small number of friends living in Paris acquired some old FX4s and also noticed other similar vehicles on the streets. They placed notes under the windscreen wipers of these cabs, asking to be contacted and if they knew where to find spare parts. One note was placed under a cab belonging to Jean-Pierre Milan, the owner of the world famous Closerie des Lilas restaurant, the haunt of such people as Picasso, Jean-Paul Sartre and Ernest Hemingway. Jean-Pierre invited the friends to a drink at the restaurant, and from that the club was formed and the name decided upon. Today the club has between 60 and 80 members.

Crazy Cabs of Paris line up outside the Closerie des Lilas restaurant on the Boulevard Montparnasse

Chapter 7
Special Bodies, Special Versions & Famous Owners

The FX4's turning circle and separate chassis are features that have appealed to specialist body builders, who at various time placed commercial bodies on specially supplied 'drive-away' vehicles, consisting of the full chassis plus front wings and windscreen and, if required front doors. Hearse bodies were supplied by Thomas Startin Ltd and Alpe and Saunders, amongst others. Gown van bodies were fitted to a few FX4 chassis, but they were not commonplace. The extra expense was not justified when all that was gained was a tight turning circle.

In the 1950s, the FX3 chassis had made a popular base for the vans delivering London's three evening newspapers, and it seemed a reasonable thing for at least one of the papers, the Evening News to order vans built on the FX4. They were nowhere near as successful as the FX3s: in fact very few were delivered. The troubles experienced with the FX4's automatic gearbox by the cab trade must also have affected the decision of the Evening News' vehicle suppliers and they were soon dropped in favour of more conventional vans.

In 1967, another British institution, the Royal Mail put an FX4 with a specially-built 200 cu. ft. mail van body on test, to evaluate its turning circle and its general capabilities. It was initially allocated to the South Eastern District Office in London in February 1967 and although no records have been located to confirm it, it was believed to have been unstable when fully loaded.

It was later sent up to Coventry, where it was used as a standard 150 cu. ft. mail van. The Post Office kept it until late 1974, or probably early 1975 to help with the Christmas post, when it was most likely sold for scrap.

An FL2 hearse from the early 1960s, built by Thomas Startin Jnr of Birmingham

45

A London Evening News van, built on an FX4 chassis. The sliding door arrangement is very crude compared to that of its FX3 predecessor

In the early 1990s, a prototype FL2 was fitted with a 2.2 litre Nissan petrol engine by Tickford, converted to run on CNG (compressed natural gas). It was tested along with several other types of vehicle to assess its performance with this type of fuel. It was later sold to an individual taxi proprietor, who had it adapted to full taxi specification, including wheelchair accessibility and ran it for several years with no trouble, even going to the expense of installing a natural gas pump in his front garden to provide a reliable supply of fuel. An LPG conversion for Fairways, by Janspeed was offered in 2000, using a 1.8-litre Rover engine, but it was not as successful as hoped. Trials begun in 1997 by LTI of an Iveco engine using LPG proved inconclusive: the fuel savings were outweighed by a shorter engine life.

The charisma of the London taxi, especially the FX4 has persuaded a number of people to buy them for their personal use. As well as there being a quite a number of old taxis sold out of service to private owners, some wealthy people bought the FL2 (and later the FX4) new, either in standard form or specially adapted to their own personal requirements.

The single FX4-based van tested by the Royal Mail

This FX4S-Plus-based FL2, brought up to taxi specifications was fitted with a 2.2 litre Nissan engine converted to run on compressed natural gas. Here it is connected to the special fuel supply rigged up in the owner's garden

For example, businessman and Conservative peer, Lord Peter Palumbo bought a 1972 FL2, one of the last petrol models to be made and had it fitted with the tinted rear window from the FX4 and an intercom. Another peer, the late Lord Winchilsea, who, besides being a descendant of the man who flag started the first London-Brighton Emancipation Run (more popularly known as the Veteran Car Run.) was the London cab trade's representative in the House of Lords kept a Fairway as his personal transport in the City of London. One particular model that made headline news in 1982 was the official car of the Governor of the Falkland Islands, Rex Hunt, when he officially surrendered to the invading Argentine armed forces.

Three 'stretch' versions have been built. One was commissioned by an anglophile American doctor, Bill Wallace from Atlanta, Georgia. Having owned a Range Rover and various Rolls-Royces he decided that a London taxi was what he next wanted. In 1984 after some lengthy correspondence and some visits to Carbodies Ltd., Dr Wallace ordered a stretch version of the revived FL2. It was built for him by Tickford Coachbuilding, then a division of Aston Martin Ltd., who inserted a 16-inch section between the front and rear doors. Known by Dr Wallace as "the Tickford", it is powered by a 2.3 litre Ford Pinto engine, fully compliant

A recent venture into LPG power came from Janspeed, who in the late 1990s transplanted a 1.8-litre Rover petrol engine into a Fairway Driver. Although savings were made on fuel consumption, the vehicle proved initially unreliable, with reports of overheating

47

Left: the Ford-powered FL2 stretch limousine, built by Tickford
Below, left: grey Connolly leather with red piping, Wilton carpet, walnut door cappings, curtains and a cocktail cabinet create a plush interior

with the then US Federal emission regulations and Ford C3 automatic gearbox, which gives it a maximum speed of 75 mph, although its cruising speed is a more modest 50mph.

A second, similar vehicle was built at around the same time by Robert Jankel Associates and a third was completed in 1986 for LTI by hearse maker Woodall Nicholson around an FX4S , to serve as a ferry vehicle for the Motor Show at the National Exhibition Centre and also as a mobile advert. It had six doors, all hinged at the front end and an additional bench seat in the passenger compartment. It was powered by a 2.5 litre Land Rover petrol engine.

One lavishly appointed limousine was supplied to His Royal Highness Prince

Six full doors mark out this stretch FX4S, built for LTI at Woodall Nicholson's factory in Bolton, Lancashire

The Fairway limousine built for the Crown Prince of Tonga gets a final polish at LTI before dispatch

Tupouto'a, the Crown Prince of Tonga. The story goes that he was using a Mercedes limousine, but the chauffeur got drunk one night and smashed it up. The Crown Prince, who had attended Sandhurst Military Academy and knew about London taxis decided to try one as a replacement. Negotiating through the Tonga High Commission, LTI built him a special version with a 2.4-litre Nissan petrol engine, leather trim, a cocktail cabinet with Brierley crystal glasses and jugs, CD player and intercom. One advantage the Fairway offered the Crown Prince was that at official functions, he did not have to remove his ceremonial sword to get into it, as he does with a saloon-based limousine. Delivered in 1996, it is understood to have cost £35,000, about half as much again as a production cab.

The actor, Sir Laurence Olivier bought an FL2 and had it trimmed in Bedford cord. He chose it as a mobile office and study because, he said he was always working with three scripts: one for his current play, one he was rehearsing and the third that he was studying. Travelling in the back of a cab gave him the privacy to read them all! Sidney James, star of the 'Carry On' films and his own series, 'Taxi' had his own privately-owned cab, as did, more recently the actor and

author Stephen Fry.

HRH the Duke of Edinburgh was another owner, although he now owns a Metrocab. Civil engineers

The FX4 has been the choice of people who want to build something different. This highly modified 1979 Austin FX4 has an 8.2-litre Chevrolet V8 and full hydraulic lift gear, which makes the cab 'dance'

49

Chris Winchilsea, the Earl of Winchilsea and Nottingham was for many years the London cab trade's representative in the House of Lords. He enjoyed owning a Fairway Driver as his personal transport

Balfour Beatty operated an FL2 limousine from their south London offices during the early 1980s.

As well as being the preferred transport of some famous people, the FX4 was the choice of some health authorities for passenger ambulances, and in most cases they served the needs well. But the most remarkable versions of the FX4 were commissioned by the flamboyant Armenian oil magnate, Nubar Sarkis Gulbenkian. Fabulously rich, he loved his cars, especially Rolls-Royces, of which he had several, all with very distinctive and showy coachwork. In the late 1950s, he decided on something different for use in London, where he had a home and did much of his business. Through Rolls-Royce dealers, Jack Barclay he ordered a special body on an Austin FX3 chassis and, according to some sources had it fitted with a Rolls-Royce engine. The body was built by FLM Panelcraft of South London and had the razor edge styling of a Victorian formal carriage. The sides were covered with basketwork similar to that of a Delaunay-Belleville owned by his mother when the family lived in Monte Carlo before the Great War. He replaced it in 1960 with an FX4, with similar coachwork, also

The third and last of Nubar Gulbenkian's remarkable taxis, made in 1966

Left: the Governor of the Falklands Islands, Rex (now Sir Rex) Hunt with his FL2 limousine. The limousine came to the public's attention when the islands were invaded by Argentina in 1982, no doubt because the vehicle was such a British icon

decorated with basketwork. His final taxi, a second FX4 delivered in 1966 cost him £3,500, more than three times the price of a basic cab. This was perhaps the least elegant, not having the proportions of the previous limousines, and the sides were painted with Regency stripes. When asked why he chose to have a taxi as his personal transport he is reputed to have said, 'it can turn on a sixpence; whatever that may be!'

On the same day he met representatives of the London cab trade at Buckingham Palace, (*see page 23*) HRH the Prince of Wales got the opportunity to drive this FX4, specially painted at Carbodies to commemorate HM Queen Elizabeth II's Silver Jubilee. A number of working cabs were also painted to commemorate the event, some entirely in silver, others with silver roofs

Chapter 8
Models and Memorabilia

People of all ages have been attracted to the London taxi, including children and the its play value in toy form is enormous. Model collectors like it too, especially since when the various forms of all-over advertising, known as liveries began to appear and model makers started reproducing them, and model railway enthusiasts find that a rank of miniature taxicabs by the stations adds interest to their carefully crafted scenery.

Model car makers, large and small have over the FX4's half-century made a large number of versions of the cab, some accurate, some less so; some for the toy market, some for the tourist market, often paired with a London bus and some for true model collectors, who demand nothing less than perfection.

And there are badges and other decorative items too. In this chapter is a selection of the many different versions of model FX4 that have been made, and a selection of the badges and other items bearing its image.

Above: three of Corgi Toys' later type of FX4, in liveries of the Financial Times, the Evening Standard and the Computer Cab logo of the 1990s
Left: an example of Corgi's original type, in 1/43rd scale

Above: three of the best 1/43rd scale FX4s. From left to right; an unknown Italian make; Somerville's white metal version and the Triang 'Spot-On'

Upper right; three of Budgie Toys' version. The right hand model was made to commemorate the 25th anniversary of the London Vintage Taxi Association

Lower right: two versions of Dinky toys' FX4, including one in Queen's Silver Jubilee livery

Below: five examples in approximately 1/76th scale, clockwise from top left: Tomica 'Stand and Post' Newspaper livery; Matchbox, 'London to Sydney Taxi Ride' livery; standard black, Corgi; standard black, Realtoy; Tomica 'Model Road & Rail' model shop logo

Maisto's superb 1/18th scale Fairway

Corgi's tinplate FX4, also in 1/18th scale has a clockwork motor

Although not as detailed as the Maisto Fairway, Polistil's 1/18th scale Austin FX4 is a very accurate representation

By contrast, newcomer Oxford Diecast's FX4 is available in 1/76th scale and also in 'N' gauge, ideal for use on model railway layouts

Not all models are white metal or die cast- this remarkably accurate model is actually made of coal!

The German firm of Hofbauer make a range of glass models and figures, including this Austin FX4

Cab drivers are always ready for a 'cuppa', so why not have a taxi tea pot?

Many items have been made with the FX4 image, including lapel badges, key rings, cufflinks and, top right a belt buckle

Appendix 1
The Public Carriage Office

London's taxis are renowned the world over for their practical, easily recognisable shape, their safety record and the expertise of their drivers. All this is due to the efforts of the licensing authority, the Public Carriage Office, who write the regulations governing the design of the cabs, inspect and license them and also license their drivers.

For most of the three centuries before the arrival of motor cabs, (which would quickly become known as taxis or taxicabs on the introduction of the taximeter) London's hackney coaches and, later the two-wheeled hansom cabs and the four-wheeled 'growlers' were licensed by the Hackney Coach Office. Then, in 1843, control was passed to the Metropolitan Police who in turn established a separate department, the Public Carriage Office, (PCO) which also, for the first time undertook to license the cabmen.

In 1891 the Public Carriage and Lost Property Offices were transferred to a new building in New Scotland Yard but in 1927 were moved to a new Metropolitan Police building in Lambeth Road, where suitable facilities for inspecting motor cabs were provided. There were also several regional 'Passing Stations', performing a similar function. However, by the 1950s, the Lambeth Road building was becoming overcrowded and so the Metropolitan Police decided that all the PCO's various departments, including the administration of cab licensing and the examiners for the Knowledge of London (the rigorous test every aspiring London cab driver has to pass before being given the coveted 'green badge') and its Passing Stations, by now four in number should be gathered under one roof.

The Public Carriage Office at Scotland Yard, off London's Whitehall, around 1884. The two cabs, the Hansom on the left and the Growler were the two types of vehicle approved by the PCO. To this day, cabmen refer to the PCO building as 'The Yard'

A new building in Penton Street, Islington was completed in 1961 and has remained the home of the PCO to the present day. Here, until 2007 cabs were presented for 'passing', i. e. the granting of a licence to work, which would last a calendar year. When a cab licence expired, the proprietor had to hand the licence plates back to the PCO and then remove the cab from the road and give it a thorough overhaul, ensuring all mechanical components are fit for service and the bodywork sound and clean. He then would take it to the PCO, where, after the Vehicle Examiner (known colloquially as a 'brown coat' because of the overall he was issued to wear or, on occasions a Senior Vehicle Examiner, known as a 'white coat') had taken it on a short road test to ensure the meter (newly fitted for the next year's licensing) was accurate, the cab would then be placed on a ramp and thoroughly inspected. If the examiner found the cab to be in order, he would give the proprietor a set of plates, one for the boot lid and another to be fixed in the passenger compartment. The cab could then be sent to work. If a cab was not found to be fit for work, the proprietor had to take it back to the garage, rectify the faults and represent it.

But the Vehicle Examiners did not just spend their time at Penton Street. Regularly they would go out on patrol, making spot checks on cabs. If an Examiner were to find a cab that was not up to scratch, he would issue an 'Unfit Notice', known colloquially as a 'Stop Note'. The cab then had to be removed from work, the fault rectified promptly and taken back to the PCO for inspection. If the work was done to the examiner's satisfaction, the 'Stop Note' was removed and the cab could be returned to work.

For years, there was no fee charged to cab proprietors for passing a cab but in the 1980s, a fee was introduced for the task and has been in place ever since. Unlike provincial taxi licenses, there is no commercial value attached to a London taxi licence plate; it remains the property of the PCO, it cannot be bought or sold and can be revoked at a moment's notice.

In 2000, control of the Metropolitan Police passed to the newly formed Greater London Authority and along with it went the PCO, which was incorporated into a new body, Transport for London (TfL) alongside London buses, the Underground, trams, Docklands Light Railway, private hire and street maintenance. The trebling of the numbers of cabs on the road from the 7000-odd in 1958 meant that in 2007 the inspection of vehicles was subcontracted to a private company, SGS, who provide this service in three locations, Hanworth, west London, Tottenham in north London and Deptford in south east London and its inspecting officers perform the same function as when they were based at Penton Street.

Appendix 2
The Conditions of Fitness

What makes London's taxis so different from any other in the world? The answer lies in a set of rules called the Conditions of Fitness. They are written by London's taxicab licensing authority, the Public Carriage Office and have been around, in a form specially written for motor cabs since 1906. Motor cars were very new then, with few people having any knowledge of how to drive or maintain them, let alone build them safely, so the PCO, as a division of the Metropolitan Police and thus guardians of public safety were faced with a dilemma: how safe would motor cabs be? Would the petrol in the tanks explode, or would one run out of control in a busy street, with unimaginable consequences? The PCO needed to set some standards and after some detailed consultation they produced, in March 1906 their first Conditions of Fitness for motor cabs, with the aim of making them safe and practical for the passengers.

There were already rules to govern the design of cars, the Motor Cars (Use and Construction) Act of 1903, but the Conditions of Fitness went further, specifying, for instance rules for the safe design of fuel tanks and of the wiring. Crucially, they included a requirement for a 25-foot turning circle so that cabs could turn without stalling and blocking the street, and also a 10-inch ground clearance, so that if a pedestrian were to be run down by a cab, he would not suffer further harm as it ran over him. The rules also required such headroom in the cab that allowed a gentleman to wear a top hat whilst seated and, if riding in a four-seat cab to allow sufficient knee room so that he might sit opposite a lady without the chance of their knees touching. Another rule, still in force demands the separation of passengers and driver. This was laid down because, in the words of Chief Superintendent Bassom, the head of the PCO who introduced the rules, " … cabs are not like private motors where the owner knows the class of person he has beside the driver, but public carriages are frequently used by persons who are more hilarious than wise … getting beside the driver and interfering with the mechanism … so as to be a source of danger to themselves and others using the roads."

The Conditions of Fitness were left unchanged until 1927, when motor car design had left them far behind, and even then, in what was a major review only introduced a reduction in the ground clearance to 7 inches. Thus, whilst cars were made lower, faster and sleeker, cabs still had an upright, stately, even antiquated appearance. Even the poor cabman was left out on the cold, with a window in the driver's door only permitted from 1938.

Before the Second World War, the landaulette body, with its drop-down hood was popular with proprietors, not because it offered fresh air in summer months, (Indeed, the smoke and fumes that filled the air in the capital were a real health hazard), but because when it was closed, it offered a great deal of privacy. This style of body was most favoured by night drivers who would pick up the 'ladies of the night', who would entertain their clients in the back of a cab while being driven around a secluded park. But such body styles were banned after the war, as the PCO wanted cabs to be more like modern cars, whilst keeping a distinct appearance.

In 1961, a second major review of the Conditions of Fitness, and the threat of their abolition came about through a challenge to the whole trade, by a certain Michael Gotla, a private hire car operator, who introduced a fleet of Renault Dauphines onto the streets. He called them minicabs and with them tried to circumvent the laws of plying for hire. A private hire vehicle may not ply for hire on the street or on a rank like a taxi; it has to be pre-booked through a third party, usually via an office, but Gotla told his drivers to use the two-way radios in the cars to make the booking with his control room. The trade was in uproar, as the minicab drivers simply took the passengers without making any sort of booking. Instead of banning minicabs, as the licensed cab trade demanded, the government set up a review of the Conditions of Fitness to see if the London taxi as the world knew it was necessary any more. This put the trade into a state of limbo and some tried to see if saloon cars could be adapted. Carbodies had a BMC Mini adapted, with a high roof and sliding doors, whilst Beardmore Motors modified a Ford Cortina by fitting a partition. In the end, the regulations were to stand, with only minor changes.

The last serious challenge to the Conditions of Fitness came in 2000, but unlike what had happened in the Gotla debacle it came from a group of people dedicated to the licensed cab trade and to purpose-built cabs but equally committed to moving the trade, and taxi design forward. They had built cabs converted from proprietary vans, complying with the Conditions of Fitness in every other way except for the turning circle and introduced them into the provincial trade. They were enjoying some success and now they wanted to bring them into London to challenge LTI's dominance of the market.

The challenge was unsuccessful as was an appeal and to date, the turning circle rule remains in place. Changing the rule may, in practice have meant the gradual replacement of cabs of a traditional appearance with those based on MPVs, a point that is currently debated: does it matter any more, or would London lose one of its real assets? The debate is not purely academic. Already, a new Mercedes-Benz cab is running in London, based on the Vito van. Whether the travelling public acknowledge it as a taxi, or not, with the possible result of buyers of the cab spending a premium price for less reward, remains to be seen.

Appendix 3
Advertising on London Taxis

Advertisements had been banned on London cabs, both internally and externally from 1886. Trade vehicles bearing adverts were banned from entering Royal Parks so as not to offend Royal sensibilities, and thus ads on horse cabs, which had access to the parks were not allowed either. As the fitting of adverts would have been optional, it would not have been acceptable to the public to have cabs without adverts being allowed in Royal Parks, but cabs with them, prohibited and thus compromising an otherwise universal service.

Opposition to internal adverts existed too: in 1910, when two-thirds of the horse cabs in London had already been supplanted by motors, an application was made to the PCO to allow a small, discreet advertisement to be fixed to the splashboard of a hansom cab. The application was refused. Further, the head of the PCO, Chief Inspector Bassom advised the solicitor representing the applicant; 'It has always held that the hirer of the hackney carriage (cab) has

the exclusive use for the time being of the vehicle, therefore he should not be forced to have a vehicle placarded with advertisements. The only safe method is to prohibit entirely.'

As a result of the changes to the Conditions of Fitness in 1927, adverts were allowed on the division bulkhead and on the

Above: a single door advert, allowed on London cabs from 1982
Left: proponents of double-door ads had to wait over a decade to see them approved
(Note: the red wheels on this particular cab indicate that it belongs to a fleet. Often this was done to identify stolen spare wheels, or at least to minimise the occurrence of theft)

backs of the two tip-seats, to try and generate some small extra income for hard-pressed cab proprietors during the Depression. Each design had to be approved by the PCO, who were mindful of passenger sensibilities. Take-up was very low at first, although after the Second World War, they became more popular.

In 1982, the Home Office, who were then in charge of the Metropolitan Police and thus the PCO relaxed their position and allowed external adverts on the front doors. A lot of the pressure for this change came from the large radio circuits, especially Computer Cab Ltd, as much of a way of identifying their cabs to their passengers as a way of advertising the company. Like the internal adverts, all external ones have to have the PCO's approval, but some advertising companies found ways around the rules to gain an an extra edge. One such example involved the tobacco producer John Player, which was sponsoring the Lotus Formula 1 motor racing team. The racing cars were painted black with the gold 'John Player Special' logo, copying the packets of that brand of cigarette, and applying that logo to the doors of an all-black cab produced a 'JPS' taxi. It is apposite that the boss of Lotus, Colin Chapman himself aroused controversy over his somewhat flexible interpretations of the rules of motor racing! The idea was taken up by the company representing the world famous London department store, Harrods, who paid for cabs to be resprayed in the store's own shade of green, with their logo on the doors. These examples were tolerated by the PCO for a while, but when pink cabs advertising the Financial Times newspaper appeared and complaints were made about them, the PCO called a halt to the practice.

However, by the early 1990s, the PCO allowed all-over advertisements, known as 'liveries'. A wide variety of imaginative and attractive designs appeared, including those for the Evening Standard, Guinness and, yes, even a pink 'Financial Times' cab. Cab proprietors take out a

'Supersides' ads cover both doors and wings, following the profile of the cabs' swage lines. Occasionally, cab adverts were used as part of a coordinated campaign, like this example for the Belgian airline, Sabena at the London City Airport

All-over liveries attracted some imaginative and colourful designs, such as this one for IBM

fixed term contract with the livery suppliers and are paid a set sum of money. When the term expires, the advertising company guarantees to return the cab to its original colour.

During the mid 1990s, permission was given to display adverts on both doors, and shortly afterwards, 'supersides' adverts, covering all four wings and doors were accepted. Cab advertising, previously banned became a recognised enterprise and both taxi garages and owner drivers are able to earn extra money having their cabs covered in this way.

The Evening Standard livery was an early example of some of the very complex designs that would be applied to cabs. Minor traffic hold-ups were said to have occurred when stationary motorists became absorbed in reading the 'pages' on the sides of these cabs!

Appendix 4
Buying a Retired FX4

Buying and running a retired London taxi has both benefits and disadvantages. As a 'hobby' vehicle they are very different from the usual Morris Minors and MGBs and they will certainly attract attention if the owner lives outside the capital, and the right model in top condition can provide a much sought-after wedding car, offering the opportunity for it to pay for itself.

Any disadvantages depend on the model of FX4 you buy and the condition it is in. The very early models, pre-1968 are very rare, partly because they rusted badly in the first place and partly because they were so noisy and draughty that few people wanted them as private vehicles. Models from the 1970s and 1980s are rare too, again for similar reasons, although rust-proofing had improved, the larger engine improved performance and the soundproofing and power steering and full servo brakes (fitted from late 1982) make them better to drive.

The best entry-level models are the Fairway and Fairway Driver. The first of these was introduced in 1989 and the great majority have now been retired from work. The virtually bomb-proof Nissan engine and automatic gearbox, along with the power steering and full servo brakes make them the smoothest, quietest and fastest model to drive. They are not sports cars by any means, but keeping up with modern traffic is no problem in a Fairway. However, these cabs will have done upwards of 400,000 miles, or more in some cases and although many components will have been replaced, sometimes more than once, there will be parts that will still need renewing. Rust is still a problem too and you must be prepared to do a certain amount of remedial work if you want to bring it to tip-top condition.

Retired examples of early Fairways can and do vary a great deal in condition. This is a very good one, sold out of the trade after being refurbished by its fleet proprietor. Others may be shabby, worn out, rust-ridden and only fit for spares

As with all old vehicles, it's good advice to buy the best you can afford and if you are not sure of what you are looking at, take someone along who does. Examples can be bought privately or through a small number of dealers, but be aware that although a dealer will sell a smart, refurbished cab with an MoT, (and for a bit more money, one with plenty of 'dress-up' parts on it) he works on a modest profit margin and will only replace what needs to be done, rather than strip down and inspect every major component. In other words, 'if it ain't broke, he won't fix it'. With regard to bodywork, it's unlikely that, for instance rusty door skins will have been replaced, but instead filled and painted to the same standard acceptable to the Public Carriage Office if it were presented for licensing. Nor will he give you a warranty- the vehicles are simply too old and there isn't the profit in the deal to underwrite one anyway.

A few words of caution: if you are an overseas buyer importing an old FX4 from Britain, do make sure that your country's laws allow you to do so and, for that matter give you the freedom to use it. For example, Federal law in the USA forbids the import of motor vehicles under 25 years old if they do not comply with very strict safety and exhaust emission laws. Law breakers, or those who have bought an illegally imported vehicle from someone who has imported it illegally risk having that vehicle seized by the Federal authorities and crushed, and they will receive no compensation. Canada is also strict on standards, but the age limit is only 15 years. German federal law now allows states to ban the use of certain 'oldtimers' that do not comply with strict emmission criteria.

Although it may seem obvious, buying an old taxi does not allow you to work it as one! (You may hire it out privately for film or wedding work, but there are other considerations such as proper insurance cover to be taken into account). Obsolete licence plates can be bought and fixed to the cab, as can old taximeters but again neither item allow you to ply for hire on the streets. Nor do the licence plates allow you to use London's bus lanes or exempt the vehicle from the Central London Congestion Charge. These are privileges granted only to properly licensed London taxis.

Some people have fitted non-standard engines into FX4s to make them better to drive. That is fine if you have the ability to do it, but if you do, make sure the new engine is not too powerful for the brakes, which were originally designed to stop the cab from just 60mph (95kpm) or the suspension, which was designed for town traffic and load carrying, not motorways or race tracks. If you are not confident about undertaking such an operation or do not have the money to pay a specialist, leave well alone. (A wise move in any case is to fit ventilated brake drums, [on all models except the Fairway Driver, which has disc brakes] which will minimise brake fade when stopping from higher speeds)

Above: one of the finest recent restorations of an FX4 was carried out on this 1972 model by its owners, Bart and Guijs de Bruijn in Holland, whilst still in their teens and at college
Left: the cab as it was when bought home by the brothers

Virtually all spare parts for the FX4 can still be bought, most of it unused, 'new/old stock' or, occasionally remanufactured stock and the biggest, most knowledgeable and most reliable supplier is a British company, Vintage Taxi Spares. (www.vintagetaxispares.com)

The best club for enthusiasts of old London taxis of all types and ages is the London Vintage Taxi Association, (www.lvta.co.uk) which has been in existence for over 30 years and offers unequalled technical expertise and advice on authentic restoration to its members. There are three main sections: one for UK members, one for members in North America and one based in Holland for members in mainland Europe. Members elsewhere in the world are administered from the UK.

Appendix 5
Production Figures & Technical Specifications

Production Figures

FX4/FL2 Chassis Production at Longbridge, Birmingham

1958/59:	216	1959/60: 1480	Total: 1,696

FX4/FL2 Chassis Production at Adderley Park, Birmingham

1960/61:	1365	1965/66:	1423	1970/71:	1591
1961/62:	738	1966/67:	1158	Total:	16,079
1962/63:	1309	1967/68:	1943	(Chassis production	
1963/64:	1282	1968/69:	1468	moved to Carbodies in	
1964/65:	1530	1969/70:	2272	1971)	

Austin FX4/FL2 Production at Carbodies, Holyhead Road, Coventry

1971:	1100	1975/76:	3122	1979:	2439
1971/72:	2833	(15 months' production		1980:	2007
1972/73:	2397	to Dec 31 1976)		1981:	2049
1973/74:	2312	1977:	2687	Total:	25,450
1974/75:	2082	1978:	2422		

Austin & Carbodies FX4/FL2, Carbodies FX4R/FL2, LTI FX4S, FX4S-Plus, Fairway & Fairway Driver Production at Holyhead Road

1982:	1864	1986:	2231	1992:	1674
(FX4, FX4R & FL2)		1987:	2128	1993:	1530
1983:	2171	(FX4S & S-Plus)		1994:	1761
1984:	1612	1988:	2332	1995:	2339
1985:	1813	(FX4S-Plus)		1996:	2558
(FX4R & FL2)		1989:	2737	1997:	2166
		1990:	3070	(Fairway Driver)	
		1991:	1846	Total:	33,832
		(Fairway)			

Grand Total (excluding 1997) 74,891

Technical Specifications

Austin FX4 & FL2: 1958-1971

ENGINE
Diesel: Austin 4-cylinder, ohv
Bore x stroke 3.25in (82.55mm) x 4in
(101.6mm)
Cubic capacity: 132.7 cu in (2178cc)
Max bhp: 55 @ 3,500rpm
Max torque: 89lb/ft @ 2,800rpm
Compression ratio: 20:1

Petrol: Austin 4-cylinder, ohv
Bore x stroke: 3.125in (79.44mm) 4.375in
(111mm)
Cubic capacity: 134.1 cu in (2199cc)
Max bhp: 55.9 @ 3,750rpm
Max torque: 112lb/ft @ 2,000rpm
Compression ratio: 7.5:1

TRANSMISSION
Automatic: Borg Warner DG150 3-speed , later
Borg Warner BW35 3-speed
Manual: (from 1961) 4-speed synchromesh on
2nd, 3rd & top gears

REAR AXLE
Hypoid, 4.8:1 final drive (Early FL2: 5.125:1)

BRAKES
Four-wheel hydraulic, dual circuit with separate
master cylinders. 11in drums all round.
Mechanical handbrake on rear wheels

SUSPENSION
Independent with coil springs and lever arm
shock absorbers on front, semi-elliptical leaf
springs with lever arm shock absorbers on rear

ELECTRICAL
12v positive earth

DIMENSIONS
Overall length: 14ft 11 7/16in (4.56m)
Overall height: 5ft 8 11/16in (1.74m)
Overall width: 5ft 8 5/8in (1.74m)
Wheelbase: 9ft 2 5/8in (2.81m)
Track, front: 4ft 8in (1.42m)
Track, rear: 4ft 8in (1.42m)
Turning circle: 25ft (7.62m)

Austin FX4 & FL2: 1971-1982 (Including Carbodies FX4)

ENGINE
Austin Diesel, 4-cylinder, ohv
Bore x stroke: 3.5in (88.9mm) x 4in (101.6mm)
Cubic capacity: 153.7 cu in (2520cc)
Max bhp: 63 @ 3,500rpm
Max torque: 109lb/ft @ 2,000rpm
Compression ratio: 20.5:1

TRANSMISSION
Automatic: Borg Warner BW35 3-speed. (Borg
Warner BW65 from 1978)
Manual: as per 1961

REAR AXLE
Hypoid, 3.909:1 final drive

BRAKES
As per above, except front-only servo from
1978)

SUSPENSION
As per 1958 model

ELECTRICAL
12v negative earth

DIMENSIONS
As per above except:
Overall length: 15ft 1/2in (4.58m) from 1977

Carbodies FX4R & FL2 London Limousine & Austin FX4Q, 1982-1985

ENGINE
FX4R & FL2 London Limousine
Land Rover diesel, 4-cylinder ohv
Bore x stroke: 3.552in (90.47mm) 3.4in
(88.9mm)
Cubic capacity: 139 cu in (2286cc)
Max bhp: 62 @ 4,000rpm
Max torque: 103lb/ft @ 1,800rpm
Compression ratio: 23:1

Land Rover petrol, 4-cylinder ohv
Bore x stroke: 3.552in (90.47mm) x 3.4in
(88.9mm)
Cubic capacity: 139 cu in (2286cc)
Max bhp: 77 @ 4,250rpm
Max torque: 124lb/ft @ 2,500rpm
Compression ratio: 7:1

FX4Q
Kalaskai diesel, 4-cylinder, ohv
Bore x stroke: 3.5in (88.9mm) x 4in (101.6mm)
Cubic capacity: 153.7 cu in (2520cc)
Max bhp: 63 @ 3,500rpm
Max torque: 109lb/ft @ 2,000rpm
Compression ratio: 20.5:1

TRANSMISSION
FX4R & FL2; London Limousine:
Automatic: Three-speed
Manual: 5-speed synchromesh
FX4Q: Automatic Borg Warner BW65 3-speed
Manual N/A

REAR AXLE
Hypoid, 3.909:1 final drive

BRAKES
Four-wheel hydraulic, dual circuit with separate
master cylinders, full servo-assistance. 11in
drums all round, Mechanical handbrake on rear
wheels

SUSPENSION
As per FX4

ELECTRICAL
Type 12v negative earth

DIMENSIONS
As per FX4 from 1978

London Coach & London Sterling, 1985-1987

ENGINE
Ford petrol, 4-cylinder, sohc
Bore x stroke: 96mm (3.781in) x 79.5mm
(3.126in)
Cubic capacity: 2302cc (140.477 cu in)
Max power 88bhp @ 4,800rpm
Max torque 118lb/ft @ 2,800rpm
Compression ratio 9:1

TRANSMISSION
Ford C3 3-speed automatic

REAR AXLE
As per FX4R

BRAKES
As per FX4R

SUSPENSION
As per FX4R

ELECTRICAL
As per FX4R

DIMENSIONS
As per FX4R except:
Overall length: 15ft 1/2in (4.58m)
Overall height: 5ft 9 1/2in (1.77m)

LTI FX4S & FX4S-Plus, 1985-1989

ENGINE
Land Rover diesel, 4-cylinder, ohv
Bore x stroke: 3.562in (90.47mm) x 3.819in
(97mm)
Cubic capacity 2495cc
Max bhp: 69.6 @ 4,000rpm
Max torque: 115lb/ft @ 1,800rpm
Compression ratio: 21:1

TRANSMISSION
Manual (both) 5-speed synchromesh
Automatic (both) Borg Warner BW40 3-speed

REAR AXLE
Hypoid, 3.909:1 final drive

BRAKES
Four-wheel hydraulic, twin leading shoe on
front. Dual circuit with tandem master cylinder.
11in drums all round, full servo-assistance.
Mechanical handbrake on rear wheels

SUSPENSION
FX4S
as per FX4R
FX4S-Plus
Front: as per FX4R
Rear: semi-elliptical glass fibre leaf springs with
telescopic shock absorbers on rear

ELECTRICAL
12v negative earth

DIMENSIONS
As per FX4R except:
Overall length: 15ft 1/2in (4.58m)
Overall height: 5ft 9 1/2in (1.77m)
Overall width: 5ft 8 7/8in (1.75m)

LTI Fairway, 1989-1992 & Fairway Driver, 1992-1997

ENGINE
Nissan diesel, 4-cylinder, ohv
Bore x stroke: 96mm x 92mm
Cubic capacity: 2663cc
Max power: 63.5kw @ 4,300rpm
Max torque: 175Nm @ 2,200rpm
Compression ratio 21.8:1

TRANSMISSION
Automatic: Nissan 4-speed
Manual: Nissan 5-speed synchromesh

REAR AXLE
Hypoid, 3.909:1 final drive

BRAKES
Fairway
Four-wheel hydraulic, twin leading shoe on
front. Dual circuit with tandem master cylinder.
11in drums all round, full servo-assistance.
Mechanical handbrake on rear wheels

Fairway Driver
Front: ventilated discs with four-pot callipers.
Rear: 10 inch drums, self-adusting. Cable
handbrake on rear wheels

SUSPENSION
Fairway
as per FX4S-Plus
Fairway Driver
Front, fully independent with double wishbones
with coils springs and telescopic shock
absorbers. Rear, semi-elliptical single leaf
springs with helper springs. (earliest models-
glass fibre leaf springs) with telescopic shock
absorbers on rear

ELECTRICAL
Type 12v negative earth

DIMENSIONS
As per FX4S-Plus

Further Reading

Bobbitt, Malcolm. Taxi! The Story if the London Taxicab. Veloce, 2002

The history of the London cab, in concise form, for the general enthusiast. P/b, b/w & colour

Garner, Simon, and Stokoe, Giles. Taxi! Frances Lincoln, 2000

A description of the London cab trade, its cabs and drivers; an ideal introduction to the subject for the general reader. H/b, b/w

Georgano, G. N. A History of the London Taxicab. David & Charles, 1972

The first modern generation book on the subject, long out of print. H/b, b/w

Georgano, G. N., and Munro, Bill. The London Taxicab. Shire Books, 2009

A pocket history of the subect. P/b, full colour

May, Trevor. Gondolas and Growlers: The History of the London Horse Cab. Alan Sutton, 1995

An in-depth academic study, but very readable. Now out of print. H/b, black & white

May, Trevor. Victorian and Edwardian Horse Cabs. Shire Books, 1999

A pocket version of the above. P/b, b/w

Merkel, Ben, and Monier, Chris. The American Taxi: A Century of Service. Iconografix, 2006

A broad history of a very large subject. P/b, b/w with some colour

Munro, Bill. Carbodies, the Complete Story. Crowood, 1998

Story of the company that became London Taxis International. Out of print H/b, b/w colour centre.

Munro, Bill. A Century of London Taxis. Crowood, 2005

In-depth history of the subject. H/b, b/w with colour centre section

Mustapha, Mus. In a Year of a London Cabbie. Orion, 2003

A collection of interviews, photographs, discussions and stories. H/b, b/w

Ward, Rod. Taxi - Purpose-built Cabs in Britain. Malvern House Publications, 2008

Pictures of cabs of all ages from around the UK. P/b, b/w with some colour

Warren, Philip. The History of the London Cab Trade. Taxi Trade Promotions, 1995

The definitive history of the subject. H/b & p/b, b/w

Warren, Philip, and Linskey, Malcolm. Taxicabs -A Photographic History. Almark, 1976

Very wide range of photographs, up to the early 1970s. Out of Print. H/b, b/w

Index